merlot

merlot

a complete guide to the grape and the wines it produces

susy atkins

MITCHELL BEAZLEY

merlot

by Susy Atkins

First published in Great Britain in 2002
by Mitchell Beazley, an imprint of Octopus
Publishing Group Limited, 2–4 Heron Quays,
London E14 4JP.

A CIP catalogue record for this book is
available from the British Library.

ISBN: 1 84000 688 9

Commissioning editor   Hilary Lumsden
Executive art editor   Yasia Williams
Managing editor   Emma Rice
Design   Nicky Collings
Editor   Colette Campbell
Production   Alexis Coogan
Index   Anne Parry

Mitchell Beazley would like to thank Oddbins in
Camden Town and Majestic Wine Warehouse in
Docklands for their help with the photography.

Typeset in RotisSansSerif

Printed and bound by
Toppan Printing Company in China

Picture acknowledgements
1, 2-3, 5 Octopus Publishing Group/Alan Williams;
6 Octopus Publishing Group/Adrian Lander; 13,
14-15 Adrian Lander/Stok-Yard; 16-17 Janet
Price; 18-19 Root Stock/Hendrik Holler; 20-21
Janet Price; 23 Art Directors & Trip/Nick Wiseman;
25 Octopus Publishing Group/Alan Williams; 26-
27 Octopus Publishing Group/Alan Williams; 28-
29 Janet Price; 30-31 Root Stock/Hendrik Holler;
33, 35 Octopus Publishing Group/Alan Williams;
36-37 Root Stock/Hendrik Holler; 39 VinVinoLife;
40-41 Octopus Publishing Group/Alan Williams;
43 Janet Price; 44-45 Octopus Publishing Group/
Jason Lowe; 47 Octopus Publishing Group/Alan
Williams; 48-49 Patrick Eagar; 50-51 Corbis/Roger
Wood; 52, 54, 55, 56-57, 58-59, 60-61, 62-63
Octopus Publishing Group/Alan Williams.

contents

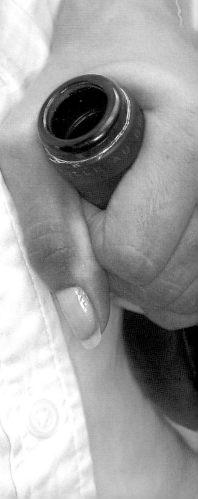

introduction

It's hard to imagine the days when Merlot was considered a poor cousin to Cabernet Sauvignon – a grape variety that would never really catch on, apart from in small pockets of Bordeaux, and even then, rarely on its own. Now it's the most fashionable red grape around and, to some wine drinkers, virtually synonymous with "red". So does Merlot deserve its new trendy image and which styles of this wine are the best and the best value? Read on...

Merlot is renowned for its wonderfully fruity, rounded, even fleshy character. So what are the factors that lead to this grape producing such wines? Here are the vine properties of Merlot.

the merlot look

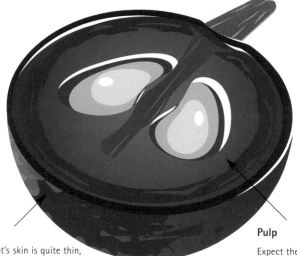

Skin

Merlot's skin is quite thin, so it is more vulnerable to rot than some varieties. The acidity level of Merlot is relatively low, although there is still a refreshing tanginess to the finished wine. Tannin levels are lower than for some red grapes. The skin is a deep colour.

Pulp

Expect the flavours of ripe Merlot (from the skin as well as the pulp) to taste of juicy red berries, particularly plums, raspberries, and cherries. There is also sometimes a hint of fruitcake and chocolate flavours. And it's useful to note the alcohol levels in Merlot are relatively high.

Leaf

This vine can quickly grow out of control and over-crop. It needs a firm hand if it's to produce low yields of good-quality grapes. Choice of site is important, and the right clone counts too – some have been developed to avoid over-cropping. Its canopy of leaves is sometimes cut back to expose the grapes more fully to the warm sunshine.

Bunch (*see* page 6)

Merlot ripens in a rush towards the end of the season and is ready for picking suddenly, so growers have to keep a careful eye on it in the autumn. If the grapes aren't ripe enough the wine will taste green and stalky. If they are too ripe on the vine they are prone to rot.

This is a grape that is grown in most red wine producing areas unlike, say, Syrah or Gamay, which are more limited to key zones. This is partly because it is seen as being hand-in-glove with the widely produced Cabernet Sauvignon, and partly because it is so popular and fashionable.

where merlot lives & why

It's also fairly easy to grow and it takes better to cooler spots than some other grapes, so winemakers use it often to fill otherwise problematic vineyards. This is why we see Merlot in Austria, northern Italy, and New Zealand.

Vineyards growing Merlot are spread throughout Europe and in most cases, these are increasing steadily. But France is its first home, and Bordeaux is the most famous region for Merlot. Here, it grows alongside Cabernet, its most common blending partner. The two flourish together throughout the region, but Merlot is the dominant vine in the St-Emilion and Pomerol areas of the Right Bank where it produces its greatest wines. Elsewhere in France, Merlot is widely seen across the southwest. France has the largest plantings of Merlot in the world, but it is also significant in Italy and Central and Eastern Europe. Since the grape became fashionable in the USA, California has seen more Merlot. There are also important tracts of Merlot in Australia, Chile, and South Africa.

Preferred soil types

Bordeaux's Right Bank areas are slightly warmer than in the Médoc on the Left Bank, but they are also prone to cold and thick clay soils. Merlot copes with that well. Soils in Pomerol sometimes have a high proportion of clay and iron; but in St-Emilion they contain more gravel and limestone – the amount of each is reflected in the wine. Clay soils, for example, are said to produce more full-bodied wines.

In Califonia, growers have tended to plant the grape in warm Central Valley locations, in order to avoid the green, under-ripe flavours that Americans so dislike. However this doesn't necessarily lead to well-balanced, subtle wines.

Merlot can produce stunning wine, but it also makes a great deal of disappointingly dull, thin plonk. This is often caused by high yields, which mean that the vine is simply producing too much fruit, and these grapes lack concentration and character. So to make a decent Merlot, winemakers must watch their yields, keeping them low enough to produce lots of plummy flavour and extract.

merlot in good hands

Ripeness is also key. Cool vineyards sometimes produce wines which have a leafy, green character. A subtle hint of this is fine, but too much can leave a wine tasting stalky and under-ripe. Winemakers control this by cutting back the canopy of leaves and exposing the grapes to the sun. Conversely, those growing fruit in hot climates must watch their fruit carefully as over-ripe grapes lead to wines that taste jammy and baked and which lack complexity.

Picking Merlot at the right moment is also important, as its thin skin means it rots relatively easily. A judicious winemaker keeps a careful eye on the climate and on the fruit for any signs of rot. And, as with all wines, good balance is everything. Big, hefty, seriously oaky Merlot may win competitions, but a silky, beguiling, ultra-fruity, rounded quality should come into the character of a great Merlot, not just power and concentration.

The partnership of Cabernet Sauvignon and Merlot is successful the world over – these grapes really do have an affinity for each other, their blends becoming, at best, more than the sum of their parts. Yet the important role Merlot plays in red Bordeaux blends often goes unnoticed by everyone except serious connoisseurs of claret. Even these traditional wine buffs used to view Merlot as the distinctly inferior partner to Cabernet Sauvignon.

merlot blends

Cabernet has traditionally been seen as the aristocrat of the two – the grape which gives the top châteaux wines their sophisticated structure, their longevity, and much of their complex personality. Merlot, on the other hand, was prized for its ability to fill out the rather austere, even tough, nature of young Cabernet Sauvignon, but it was clearly seen as helping the Cabernet along, rather than adding its own beguiling character to the mix.

Nowadays Merlot has many more fans and the predominantly Merlot-rich blends of St-Emilion and Pomerol are lauded in their own right. These blends are often a high proportion of Merlot with Cabernet Franc and less Cabernet Sauvignon. They can be long-lived, just like the Cabernet-heavy wines of the Médoc and Graves, but they tend to be more approachable when young, and their ripe fruitiness appeals to wine drinkers brought up on New World, fruit-forward styles. Meanwhile, the role of Merlot in more classic Médoc blends (perhaps with a sprinkling of Petit Verdot and Malbec in the mix, like salt and pepper) continues, but overall more Merlot is being used in Bordeaux, to produce wines that are softer and more easy-drinking in their youth. In Tuscany Merlot is sometimes successfully blended with local grape Sangiovese (see page 28). The Aussies prefer blending their Cabernet with Shiraz, although some Bordeaux-style blends do exist. Blends with Cabernet Sauvignon are available from most Merlot producing countries - try South African or New Zealand examples for a taste of top New World versions of Bordeaux. The Americans make some serious Cabernet/Merlot blends too – their Bordeaux-style wines sometimes go under the name Meritage.

The word Merlot is said to derive from the French for the blackbird – "*merle*" – which eats its ripe berries. Not a great deal more is known about Merlot's origins, but it was first associated with the Libournais region on the Right Bank of the Dordogne river, and was thriving there by the end of the eighteenth century.

how merlot grew up

By the middle of the nineteenth century it had been planted widely in the Médoc area where many of the most famous Bordeaux châteaux are located and was already noted for its ability to blend well with Cabernet Sauvignon.

Gradually its tendrils spread throughout the region – into Graves, Bourg, Blaye, Fronsac, and wider environs that produce basic, generic Bordeaux *rouge*. It became common

throughout the southwest, in Bergerac and further south in the Languedoc. There was a particular surge in plantings in the mid- to late-twentieth century as many producers turned away from white varieties and started planting more quality red. Today Merlot is more widely planted in southwest France than Cabernet Sauvignon.

Italy and Eastern Europe have had Merlot plantings since anyone can remember. However, it was not until the late twentieth century that the New World wine countries, and California in particular, became enamoured of this grape. Washington State, too, has recent huge vineyards of Merlot. Australia has been slower to get going with this grape but now seems to be turning its attention towards it a little more.

When a grape enjoys as much of a fashionable image as Merlot currently does, it's difficult to predict what will happen next. The Californians – its biggest fans over the past ten years – seem to be turning to the next big thing, be that the Rhône or Italy. But Merlot is too popular to become reviled. It might not remain the hippest grape variety on the West Coast for much longer, but my guess is that it will retain many fans there.

what will become of merlot?

As long as quality is kept fairly high, that is. Too many over-oaky, mundane-tasting Merlots and the world really *will* go off this vine. But that's unlikely. While there will always be disappointing Merlot, you could argue that there will always be bad wines made from any grape. And across the world, winemakers' understanding of what makes a good Merlot (the right soils, the right climate,

the right clones, canopy management, well-judged oak) is increasing, so better wines in general should be the result. And if the craze for Merlot ebbs a little, at least we will be left with winemakers who really care about it.

The New Zealanders and South Africans should continue to make progress with wines from this grape, or with blends that include Merlot. These are early days for premium Merlot from both countries, so we can look forward to better. Chile will continue to distinguish Merlot from look-alike Carmenère (see page 42), and hopefully concentrate on making more premium wines that show each to its best advantage. Another hope is that Eastern and Central Europe will get to invest more in their vineyards and wineries and develop their Merlot plantings. And perhaps Australia will try harder too.

Only two worries – uninspiring or plain poor Merlot from the southwest of France, Bordeaux in particular, is truly disappointing and will continue to be so until the Bordelais reduce yields and look at getting more concentration and flavour into their cheaper wines. And let's hope the over-blown, over-oaked styles of some New World wineries are toned down somewhat in the future.

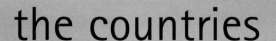

the countries

Styles of Merlot vary widely across the world. Fruit picked from a cool vineyard in Northern Italy makes quite different wine to that made from grapes grown in a warm New World area. Pin down a region's climate, its soils, and traditions, and you are halfway to recognizing the sort of Merlot to expect.

Despite the rise of New World Merlot, Bordeaux is still the grape's spiritual home and for many, the wines from St-Emilion and Pomerol remain the benchmarks for this variety. But French Merlot isn't just about names and prices.

france

If you want to understand Merlot, you had better start in France. Whatever great strides are made in the rest of the winemaking globe, Bordeaux, on France's western Atlantic coast, remains the most fascinating and telling region for Merlot. Here you will see many different faces of this wine – magnificent blends where Merlot plays a supporting or leading role, but, sadly, it's the source of much of the disappointing Merlot you will come across. Here is our grape, then, in all its manifestations, except perhaps the ultra-fruity, summer pudding style of warm New World vineyards. When red Bordeaux starts to get that fruit-forward and modern in style, it causes great controversy.

Much of the Merlot found in Bordeaux is a classic blend with the varieties Cabernet Sauvignon, Cabernet Franc, and (less important players, these) Petit Verdot and Malbec. The dominant grapes are Cabernet Sauvignon and Merlot, which is (or should be) one of the greatest double acts in wine – the rather austere, tough Cabernet fleshed out with the more generously fruity, plump Merlot. The Cabernet component has traditionally been more celebrated, with

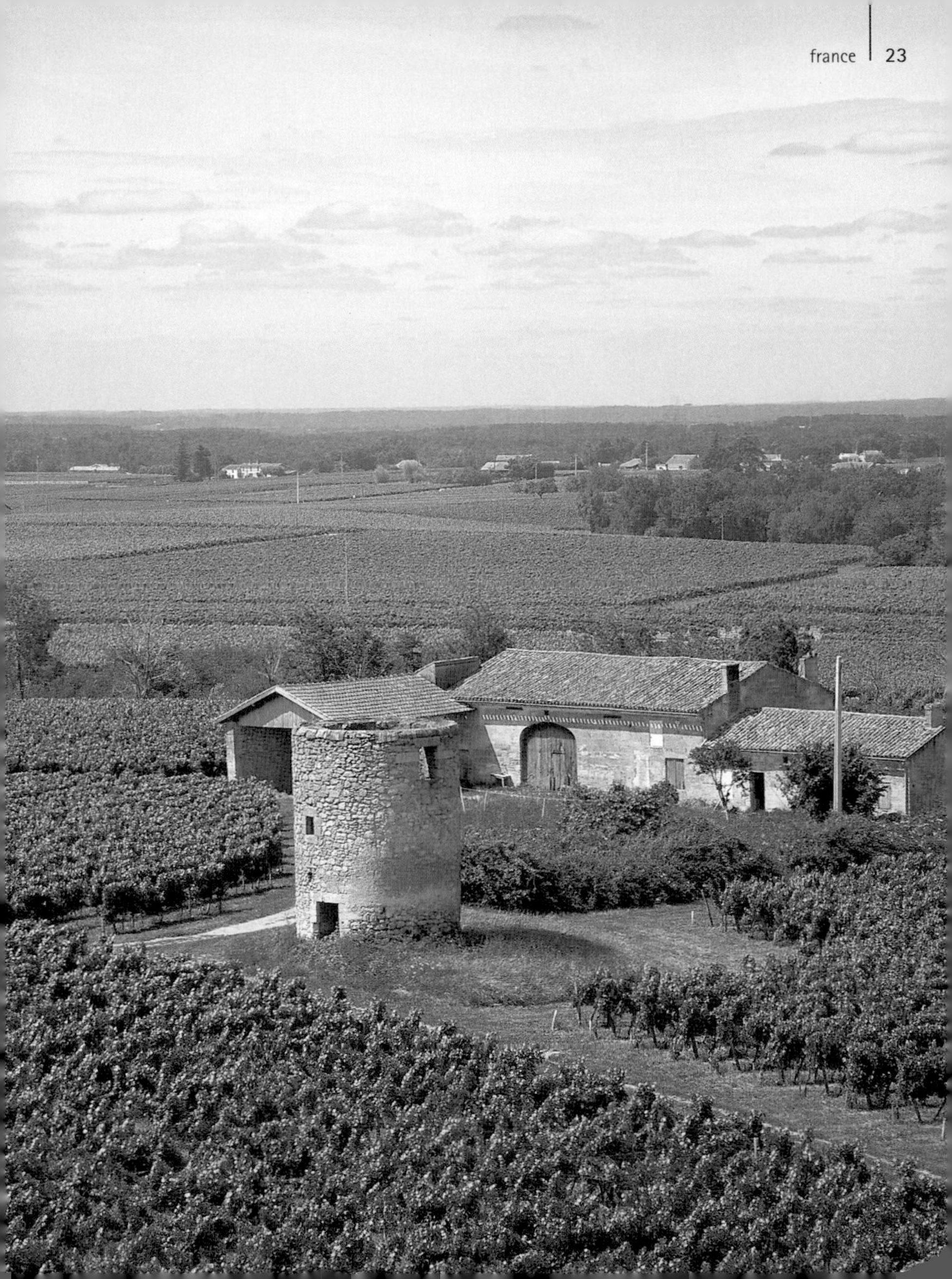

The AC system

Merlot treated as second best until recently, when a trend for softer, more fruity wines became apparent. Gradually, drinkers were starting to demand wines which could be enjoyed when younger, wines that didn't need decades in a cool, dark cellar to mellow and soften down. Merlot began to be very fashionable around the world, so the effect in Bordeaux was easy to predict – more Merlot started going into the blends, and its role in creating velvet-smooth, perfumed, intense clarets became more widely appreciated.

Now Merlot takes up over half the plantings in Bordeaux. Expect basic Bordeaux *rouge* and superior wines made in the outlying areas (such as the Côtes de Blaye and Bourg) to produce wines with more Merlot in them than Cabernet. These vary widely in quality, from jammy, dilute, bland, and disappointing Merlot at its most uninspiring to, in the case of the "Côtes", sometimes finely oaked, well-balanced, good-value claret.

The blends in the wines of the Graves, and the Médoc, on the Gironde's Left Bank, where the most famous villages are found (Margaux, Pauillac, St-Julien, St-Estèphe) are heavier in Cabernet (Merlot might typically be just twenty-five per cent of the wine) – which produces superb grapes in the well-drained, gravelly soil. Merlot plays an important part here, for sure, but the Cabernet element is dominant. For fine Bordeaux red that does showcase our grape head to the Right Bank and the Libournais area to St-Emilion and Pomerol. Here you can expect the proportion of Merlot to rise to sixty per cent and upwards in a blend – some wines even use one

hundred per cent. Cabernet Franc is often the main blending partner, and Cabernet Sauvignon plays a more minor role.

The result is magnificent Merlot-rich blends, heavy with ripe, generous fruit, truffles, and chocolate; aromatic, less tannic and more lush than Médoc wines; and ready to drink when younger (up to a decade younger). Some of the most celebrated wines of Pomerol, where Merlot is often eighty per cent or ninety per cent of the blend, command scarily high prices. These are made in small quantities and worldwide demand is great, so prices have shot up to almost crazy levels. At its best, though, Pomerol is wonderful wine, rounded yet well-structured, without the heavy jamminess criticized in some top New World Merlots. In part, this is due to the iron-rich clay soil that results in superbly concentrated wines.

In St-Emilion, it's more difficult to generalize about the proportion of Merlot in a blend – more Cabernet Sauvignon and Franc are often used, although Merlot is still the most important grape variety. There are lots of smaller scale winemaking operations here, as opposed to large grand châteaux, and recently there has been a proliferation of so-called "*vins de garage*" – wines that could be made in the garage– and the "*garagistes*" have become celebrated. The result is a vast number of individual styles. As with the rest of Bordeaux, the best way forward is to identify a name you like and stick with it. Look out for wines from the villages surrounding St-Emilion also, and try other wines from the Libournais such as the Côtes des Francs and Côtes de Castillon, too. Sadly, the very cheapest red Bordeaux, and that includes many own-label cheapies, should be avoided.

In the rush to sample Bordeaux's offerings, don't miss Merlot from other parts of France – this is one of the country's most widely planted red grapes and it turns up in regions as diverse as Languedoc-Roussillon, the Charente, Dordogne, and the Ardèche. Sometimes it seems that anywhere you go in France, except Burgundy and the Rhône, you may be offered a simple local wine, sometimes appealing, other times disappointingly thin and stalky, that is made from Merlot. The best bets are from the South West (especially Bergerac, the Côtes de Duras, and Côtes du Marmandais), and the Languedoc where Vins de Pays d'Oc made from Merlot and Merlot blends are usually satisfyingly rich and fruity, made in the forward, sunny, New World style. A few more serious, longer-lived, oaky Merlots and Merlot blends are made here in the Languedoc, too.

Merlot is an important grape in Italy but the quality and style can vary a great deal. If you pick up a cheap bottle of Italian Merlot, it is most likely to have come from the north of the country, and it may be faintly disappointing – a light, slightly grassy red with a vague hint of red-berry jam.

italy

Top producers

Avignonesi
Castello di Brolio
Castello di Fonterutoli
Costanti
Gaja
Ornellaia
Planeta

The problem is that Merlot is seen often in the north as a vine that can produce a high volume of everyday plonk, and it wasn't always planted in the best sites. Even the clones of the vine that were used were often the high-cropping ones. So a lot of Merlot made in Friuli, Veneto and Trentino-Alto Adige is lean stuff, perhaps grown on fertile plains, and generally not taken too seriously, although a slightly chilled glass on a hot summer's day can be refreshing. That said, the occasional richer, riper wine appears, usually from better vineyards of Friuli at the eastern edge of the country near Slovenia, and made in much smaller quantities.

Further south, in Tuscany and Umbria, Merlot is considered very fashionable and it appears both as a single varietal wine and in blends (usually with Tuscany's main grape, Sangiovese, to flesh it out and add richness). Plantings of Merlot are increasing throughout the region, notably in the super-trendy, warm coastal area Maremma. It does produce some impressively rich and well-structured Tuscan wines, but not everyone agrees that Tuscan producers should be pulling out old vineyards of native varieties to plant yet more Merlot. You won't find Merlot much in the deep south of Italy, although a few rounded, smooth, fruity wines have appeared recently from Sicily.

Top producers cont.

Le Pupille
Tua Rita
Umani Ronchi
Settesoli

The DOC system

In Italy, DOC wines are those of controlled origin, from specific regions, made with specified grape varieties and to regulated styles – it's the equivalent of French AC (*see* page 24). DOCG indicates even stricter controls, but neither DOC nor DOCG guarantee top quality. IGT is the equivalent of *vin de pays*.

Merlot isn't the most important red grape in Spain. This is a country that has concentrated on its own grape varieties (particularly Tempranillo), or turned to some extent towards Cabernet Sauvignon. That said, Merlot has started creeping in a bit more to Spanish vineyards.

spain

Top producers

Castillo de Monjardin
CoViSa
Marques de Monistrol
Palacio de la Vega
Raimat
Miguel Torres

The region of Navarra, a neighbour to Rioja in the north, is now a major producer of modern red wines and Merlot, perhaps inevitably, has started to crop up here, either on its own or in blends. Expect no great complexity but generally pleasant, juicy, medium-bodied wines – great with a plate of Spanish *jamón* (ham).

In Catalonia, the Penedès DO is another important source of Merlot. This area became hip and happening back in the 1960s when young Miguel Torres started planting international grape varieties for the first time here. The legacy today is plenty of Cabernet, Chardonnay, and, of course, Merlot, in the vineyards – wines made in a modern, international style are the result.

Further northwest, in the foothills of the Pyrénées, Aragón's Somontano DO is more newly fashionable today, and winemakers here are at the cutting edge of modern Spanish winemaking. Merlot is one of the permitted red grape varieties. Wines from Somontano tend to be "new wave" in style, ripe and fruity, and well-balanced, sometimes made from just one grape, or sometimes blends using traditional Spanish grapes mixed with French ones. Some are oak-aged for more structure. These wines are well worth a try.

Look out, too, for other regions such as Bierzo and Conca de Barberà – Merlot is being grown (sometimes experimentally) in nooks and crannies across Spain.

The DO system

In Spain, DO wines are those of controlled origin, from specific regions, made with specified grape varieties and to regulated styles – it's the equivalent of French AC (see page 24). DOCa indicates even stricter controls, but neither DO nor DOCa guarantee top quality. *Crianza*, *Reserva*, and *Gran Reserva* indicate oak ageing.

Remember when cheap Bulgarian reds took the world by storm? It was only ten to twenty years ago, but today the Merlots and Cabernets of this former Eastern bloc country have fallen out of favour, replaced by the more reliable, softly fruity charms of New World wines.

the rest of europe

Top producers

Bulgaria: Damianitza
Haskovo
Stara Zagora

Austria: (be aware that some of Austria's supposed Merlot has recently been identified as Cabernet Franc)
Pöckl
Umathum
Stiegelmar (Juris)

Greece: Kir-Yanni
Lazaridis
Domaine Spiropoulos
Tselepos

The New World producers are partly to blame for Bulgaria's lack of popularity, but then there's the terrible state of Bulgaria's wine industry since the process of privatization started. It's been beset by problems, mainly a chronic shortage of funding and endless wrangles over ownership. The inevitable result is distinctly patchy quality. Yep, Bulgarian Merlot is, if anything, less dependable than it used to be.

Still, there are some pleasant, palatable wines around. The best are very modern and straightforward in style – clean, fruity, and easy-drinking; with cherry/berry/plum flavours and often some fairly overt, spice 'n' vanilla oak (French or American, the latter has more vanilla flavour). And most Bulgarian Merlot is heart-warmingly cheap, so find a gem and buy it for parties or bargain boozing. Let's hope for more premium offerings in the future. The Struma Valley and Thracian Valley regions in the south and southwest are the most promising for reds with more structure and ageing ability than those everyday quaffers.

Hungarian Merlot can be appealing, if not terribly exciting – it's also reasonably priced, but a bit dilute and lacking in body to be deeply memorable. There's little Merlot made in Slovenia and Macedonia, but in Romania, this is a widely planted grape, once again used to produce ordinary wine rather than serious stuff. If you're going to try Romanian Merlot, buy one from the high-altitude Dealul Mare ("big hill") region in the southeast Carpathian hills, a good area for soft, ripe, better-quality reds.

Of all the countries mentioned here, Moldova has the most potential, with fine soils, a good climate, and vineyards of classic varieties. One day it is likely to wow the rest of the world with its reds, Merlot included, but for now the investment is not quite there. Watch out for it in the future.

There are some Merlot vines in Austria, and producers here like the fact that it will ripen better than Cabernet in cooler sites. Most of this fruit goes into surprisingly chunky, ripe, and firm-bodied Bordeaux-style blends, mainly from the warm Burgenland area of the country. Experimentation continues apace – watch out for Austrian reds which look exciting right now.

Merlot from Greece? Yes – after all, this country has the right natural conditions, it just lacked a modern wine industry. Now that's changing, as small-scale, family owned wineries turn their attention to up-to-date styles (not just Retsina and sweet reds). Most Merlot appears blended, possibly with Cabernet, possibly with Greek grapes. The latter are more unusual and interesting wines to sample.

There's a perception that Australia, so famous for its rich reds, makes a lot of top-grade Merlot. In fact, it doesn't go for this grape nearly as much as it does Shiraz (Syrah) or Cabernet, or indeed Pinot Noir, Grenache, and even Mataro (Mourvèdre), if some producers can be believed. Talk to Aussies and, with one or two exceptions, they don't exude huge enthusiasm for Merlot. Not nearly as much as the Californians, Chileans, and New Zealanders do, at any rate.

australia

Top producers

Balnaves
Cape Mentelle
Cullen
Devil's Lair
Grant Burge
Heggies
Knappstein Lenswood
Nepenthe
Plantagenet (Omrah)
Shaw & Smith
Tatachilla

This seems a bit strange, although it's perhaps because Australians like their reds to have a powerful structure, loads of body and extract (summed up memorably as "a lot of grunt" by one winemaker). Perhaps Merlot is too fleshy and fruity, not grunty enough! Still, plantings are slowly on the increase and Merlot may yet make more impact. Parts of Western Australia (Margaret River, Pemberton) and Coonawarra already grow decent Merlot, no surprise as these are great places for Cabernet. Now the coolish Yarra Valley in Victoria, Adelaide Hills in South Australia, and the newly emerging region of Orange in New South Wales, are coming up with fine, well-balanced Merlot and Merlot blends.

Ah yes, blends. Merlot may not appear often on its own in Oz, but it makes a valuable contribution to Australian red blends. It is usually paired with Cabernet Sauvignon (unsurprisingly, although Cabernet/Shiraz blends are much more common); sometimes with Cabernet Franc and Malbec, too. Many of the top blends – the most supple, intense yet elegant – hail from Margaret River, south of Perth. Here Francophile producers aim for Bordeaux-like finesse. The wines taste a bit too fruit-forward and bold for that, but the best are refined and they age well too. And yes, they are usually worth their high price tags.

New Zealand is more famous for its white wines than red, and for its expressive, pungent Sauvignon Blanc in particular. But don't be fooled into thinking the reds are second rate – they can be impressive, and the top Merlots and Merlot blends are among the best.

new zealand

Top producers

Craggy Range
Esk Valley
Goldwater
Matua
Sileni
Stonyridge
Trinity Hill
Unison

It wasn't always so. Many of New Zealand's winemakers have struggled to get properly ripe, concentrated reds in their relatively cool climate, and the results have all-too-often been wines with an unpleasantly "green" character – hints of green bean or grass dominating. Cabernet Sauvignon suffered the most and earlier ripening Merlot has recently been viewed as a better bet. Still, Merlot could be disappointing, too, as could Bordeaux-inspired blends of the two (perhaps with some Cabernet Franc

and/or Malbec in support). Those that succeeded with these wines were the producers in hot-spots such as warm Waiheke Island, out in Auckland harbour.

Now the Kiwis have got to grips with reds. Increasingly, they are concentrating their efforts with Merlot (and Cabernet) on the top sites where the grapes can achieve full ripeness, and they are managing their vines better in the cooler areas. Merlot is now seen as a very exciting grape here, producing some surprisingly richly fruity, chocolatey wines with good, firm structure. Ditto the Bordeaux-style blends – they are displaying the kind of concentration and body that make their high prices seem more justified.

One of the most interesting areas for Merlot is the well-established Hawke's Bay region, on the east coast of the North Island. Within Hawke's Bay, the Gimbletts Road gravel-rich area is turning out the top reds. Other fine Merlots are coming from Auckland and even cooler Marlborough on the South Island.

In the USA there has been a Merlot rush of late, with consumers crazy for the variety ever since a television programme informed them that drinking red wine in moderation was good for the health. Merlot was the grape they turned too.

north america

Top producers

Beringer
Duckhorn
Flora Springs
Matanzas Creek
Newton
Peter Michael
Shafer

California

Merlot madness gripped California in the 1990s – in part because the American market wanted some premium (or near-premium) quality red that was softer and more approachable when young than tough Cabernet; and partly because it became widely held that moderate red-wine drinking was healthy. Now the fever has died down a bit (Syrah is a new craze, for example), and even the most obsessed fan will admit that West Coast Merlot varies a great deal in quality and value for money.

Still, a top-ranking Californian Merlot can be quite brilliant, probably bettered only by one from a very good estate in Bordeaux. There are lush, ripe plums, and cherries galore; firm but rounded tannins; the sheen of fine, well-judged new oak; a hint of cream and spice perhaps... some are hefty and powerful and may last ten years or more, emerging mellow and chocolatey. The best West Coast Bordeaux-style blends are also up there – world-class wines that mature with grace. But there are plenty of wines that are more mundane, even sweet-tasting, with

a confected red-cherry flavour, and a little too much vanilla-and-coffee new oak. And others still that can taste a little green and mean and over-cropped. So don't be fooled into thinking Californian Merlot is all top-drawer stuff – much of it is nothing special at all, although truly dreadful ones are rarely encountered, thank goodness. Choosing a reputable producer is important here – oh, and then you'll have to watch those collector's wines, cult labels with price tags to match. It's all worth it when you pick a gem.

Parts of the Napa Valley, such as Stags' Leap, or Howell Mountain, have long been considered the best sites, although cooler spots like Carneros (which is in both Napa and Sonoma counties) and further flung regions such as Monterey, Mendocino, and Alexander Valley are now making good progress. Much of the lower quality, dilute Merlot from California is made in the hot, irrigated Central Valley – avoid it.

Pacific Northwest

Washington State is a promising source of Merlot. This
corner of northwest America may not be overwhelming
the shop shelves just yet but its wines are attracting more
fans, mostly for their lively, pure fruit flavours. Merlot is
planted extensively in the state's vineyards (which include
the desert-like Columbia River Valley, where vast, irrigated,
circular green plantings yield good-quality grapes) – only
overtaken in sheer numbers of vines by Chardonnay. Some
pleasingly rich and carefully oaked Merlots have issued
from Washington State – but a rather simple, fruity,
albeit pleasant wine is the norm. It would be great to see
more serious Merlots start to appear, but at the moment
winemakers here seem far more interested in creating
premium Syrah.

Apart from Californian versions and the odd Washington
gem, the best Merlot in America must come from New
York State's Long Island. Several smallish, up-market
wineries are trying their best with the variety, coming
up with some rich, ripe, and rounded wines. Which is great
– as long as you can find them. Such proximity to New
York City means that most of them are lapped up by the
metropolis or by weekenders in Long Island's Hamptons.
Little is exported.

Top producers

Washington State:
Andrew Will
Hedges
Delille
Leonetti
Chateau Ste Michelle

Long Island: Bedell
Lenz
Pelligrini

Q: When is Merlot not Merlot? A: When it's Chilean Carmenère!
It must have come as a shock for Chile's winemakers to
discover, in the 1990s, that the vine they were certain was
Merlot turned out to be, in many cases, the obscure Carmenère.
Most people hadn't even heard of this grape - it comes from
Bordeaux originally, but is almost extinct there. Chile, it now
appears certain, has it in abundance.

south america

Top producers

Chile: Caliterra (Seña)
Casa Lapostolle
Concha y Toro
Cousiño Macul
Errázuriz
Montes
Mont Gras
Santa Carolina
Villard
Vina Carmen

Chile

The Carmenère situation was especially galling for the
winemakers since Merlot was one of the main reasons for
the soaraway success of Chilean wine in the late twentieth
century. Soft, bright purple, abundantly fruity wine oozing
fresh cherry and blackcurrant was always going to be
popular; it helped, of course, that the price was usually
low, the quality pretty reliable, and the labels often
appealingly modern and easy to read. Along with Cabernet,
Merlot was one of the darlings of the Chilean wine
industry. Now it is estimated that those large Merlot
plantings are, in fact, sixty per cent Carmenère.

Who cares as long as the wines are good? The
consumer, for one, who perhaps prefers the familiar word
Merlot on a label rather than Carmenère. Interestingly,
now the discovery has been made, the Chileans are taking
Carmenère seriously, and producing wines that show more

obvious distinction between the two. Carmenère appears to be a little more full-bodied and perfumed, with an overtone often described as "soy", while Chilean Merlot continues to be seductively soft and sweetly ripe, with a hint of red- and black-fruit pastilles about it. Try both varieties if you can – at least these days you are more likely (although not certain) to know what's in your bottle. Accuracy over labelling should increase as time goes by.

One complaint about Chilean Merlot is that although it's great stuff in the cheap to medium price brackets, it rarely achieves great heights (the same is muttered about Chilean Cabernet). Well, there *is* more premium wine on the scene than ever before, and some flagship releases are serious indeed – with more concentrated and complex flavours, finer and more careful use of oak, and perhaps more emphasis on regional character. But they are expensive and anyway, there aren't enough of them. Overall, the old gripe is still valid – there is a danger that Chile will remain predominantly a producer of easy-drinking Merlot that could even become bland and

boring if one was forced to drink it endlessly. Let's hope producers aim for more and better "reserve" wines to wow us with, as well as churning out those cheaper, cheerful quaffers.

Merlot is mainly seen on its own, but it's sometimes blended, usually with Cabernet Sauvignon or Cabernet Franc, and these blends are often the result of a winery working with a Bordelais consultant or spending time in Bordeaux watching how it is done. Both blending partners work well in this country and a handful of serious, well-oaked wines is starting to emerge, although I still hanker after the bright purity of fruit flavour that one hundred per cent Chilean Merlot provides.

The grape is widely planted in several major wine regions, but many consider the Central Valley zone of Rapel, south of Santiago (subzones of which are Cachapoal and Colchagua), to be the best for Merlot. Further north, the cool Casablanca Valley shows great promise for this variety. In truth, it's more important to pick a top producer than it is to go by region.

Chilean Merlot may have had its problems, as we have just seen, but the good-value, juicy examples it produces have nevertheless won many drinkers over to South American reds. So what about the neighbouring countries?

Argentina

Argentina has concentrated primarily on Malbec. It has become a "signature" grape for the country, and is rarely seen anywhere else. But Argentina's legacy of European settlers means it has a number of other, internationally known red varieties, including Merlot, and results are encouraging. Merlot (grown in several regions including Mendoza and cooler, southern Río Negro) is used in blends (with Cabernet, Malbec, even Syrah), and on its own, and can be smooth with a black-cherry note.

The potential is for greater things, as the vineyards are mature, and winemakers are only turning their attention to this grape now, having been distracted by Cabernet Sauvignon in the past. Perhaps Chile should watch out!

Uruguay

Uruguay has its own (almost) unique selling point, Tannat, which makes big, powerfully tannic, and leathery reds. But some progress is being made with Merlot, which is sometimes used as a blending partner for Tannat, softening it up a bit and adding some fresh fruitiness.

Until recently, no one took much notice of South African Merlot, not even the producers, who had little of it in their vineyards and seemed generally uninspired by it. Sure, Merlot cropped up in the Cape's Bordeaux-style blends, some of which have long impressed, but Merlot wasn't exactly hip and happening here. Too many wines were unbalanced in some way – either over-blown and too oaky, or rather acidic.

south africa

Suddenly, it's all change as this grape variety has started to produce some startlingly good wines while simultaneously becoming one of the most fashionable varieties in the country (and world). One big advantage today's winemakers have is that they can use better clones of the vine, replacing old, virus-infected vineyards that had caused serious problems in the past. And the more progressive winemakers (a new post-apartheid generation that has witnessed the advances made elsewhere in the world and been influenced by them) are making efforts to create wines with better balance – less astringent and acidic, more ripe and rich, more judiciously oaked and less overwhelmingly alcoholic.

The regions of Stellenbosch and Paarl – traditionally the Cape's best red wine areas – are turning out the highest number of fine Merlots and Merlot blends. The best wines are typically rather big, meaty, and rich, but well-made with fine oak. It is interesting to note that several winemakers working in these regions are serious Francophiles, and they aim at Pomerol-style wines. Look out too for some concentrated, berry-dense Merlots appearing from other less-famous regions, particularly the more westerly Malmesbury.

South Africa makes some fine Cabernet, and its almost unique Pinotage is improving. But in Merlot and Bordeaux-style blends, it has another two wines in which it can excel.

Top producers

Boschendal
De Toren
Delaire
Grangehurst
Jordan
K.W.V. (Cathedral Cellar)
Longridge (Sejana)
Meerlust
Meinert
Mulderbosch
(Faithful Hound)
Plaisir de Merle
Spice Route
Steenberg
Warwick Estate (Trilogy)
Yonder Hill

As Merlot's popularity has increased, so have the number of countries keen to make premium wine from it. Keep an eye on North Africa as new investment in Merlot vineyards starts to produce decent wines, finally. Israel, India, and even the Far East are starting to make an effort with our grape, too.

the rest of the world

Moroccan wine is also worth trying, and keeping an eye on, as standards pick up for the first time in fifty years. Some new, better blends of Merlot with other reds should be among the benefits of new, usually French, investment.

Malta is a surprising source of decent Merlot. Holiday-makers have increasingly stumbled across attractive, medium-bodied Merlot and Merlot-based reds on the island, even if they are rarely available elsewhere.

In Israel, some serious Merlots and Merlot/Cabernets are now emerging, particularly from the relatively cool, high-altitude Golan Heights and Upper Galilee regions. Again, new investment is helping things along, with the result that modern, New World look-alikes packed with fresh-berry fruit are emerging from boutique wineries to take their places alongside flash-pasteurized, widely available kosher wines.

Lebanon has plantings of Merlot, as it does of most of the classic French varietals, although this is not one of the components of the world-famous Chateau Musar, where Cabernet Sauvignon is blended with Cinsault and Carignan instead.

Merlot has even stretched its tendrils as far as China, India, and Japan, where a new fondness for wine has led to plantings of, in particular, the classic varieties. Quality can be remarkably high - but it can also be dire and in any case, quantities are minute as yet.

Top producers

Israel: Castel
Galil Mountain
Recanati
Yarden

India: Grover Vineyards

120

Santa Rita M.R.

Merlot
2000
VALLE DEL RAPEL

buying, storing, & serving

The next step is buying a bottle of Merlot and deciding whether to drink it straightaway or cellar it. Here are some tips, and more information on how and when to serve it. And here you'll also find out which dishes make the best partners for wines made from this grape.

Anything as fashionable as Merlot, whether it's a designer handbag or a pedigree dog, is going to command worryingly high prices. Buyer beware!

quality vs price

Merlot is being hyped a great deal at the moment, and some of the cult labels (and would-be cult labels) cost a ridiculous amount of money. The wines may taste good, but do they taste *that* good? One-hundred-dollars good? Before you part with that kind of money for a top Pomerol or California Merlot, think about how many bottles of equally delicious but less fashionable red wine you could be buying for the same amount. Or, indeed, how many bottles of perfectly decent Merlot from a less trendy part of the winemaking world.

Then again, cheap claret makes no sense. If you're going to buy Bordeaux, think fairly expensive (but not necessarily at the very top), as the "bargains" are often disappointingly jammy, or stalky and dilute. For better value at the lower end of the price spectrum, turn to Merlot from elsewhere in the southwest of France, and the Vin de Pays d'Oc Merlot.

Then there's the odd bargain that really does taste good from Central and Eastern Europe – but these are quite the opposite of fashionable. However, Bulgarian

Merlot can be great value for money, as long as you pick a reliable source. South Africa is another tip for value-for-money Merlot. Prices in the Cape may be set to rise as the excellent reds become more widely appreciated but at the time of writing, there were plenty of excellent, under-priced Merlots and Bordeaux blends around.

Chile is still producing highly palatable, reliable Merlot at a reasonable price, too. It may not be the very cheapest, but for the amount of rounded, ripe flavour you get for your money, Chilean Merlot can impress. Then there's Argentina, snapping at Chile's heels with a relatively new surge of Merlot, mainly in the form of blends. Argentinian styles can be well priced.

New Zealand's wines are never dirt cheap, and that goes for their Bordeaux blends above all else. The top labels from Hawke's Bay and Waiheke Island, in particular, will set you back a bit, although they can be first-rate.

The really scary price tags, however, are attached to the cult Californian and Bordeaux wines. Be prepared to shell out very serious money indeed for wines that will typically be big, rich, and immature. If you have the loot to spend, the cellar to store the wine, and the patience to wait for years while the wines reach their peak, then go ahead. But ordinary mortals may want to hold back – there are better-value Merlots out there, honest!

Don't imagine that if you like Merlot you will love Cabernet Sauvignon. These are quite different varieties and blend well precisely because they *are* so different (*see* page 14). Merlot-mad wine drinkers are far more likely to enjoy medium-bodied wines made from juicy, red-fruity grapes.

other wines to try

Try Grenache. It might not have the finesse of a good Merlot, but the Grenache grape (known in Spain as Garnacha) has the same ripe sense of summer berries. Go for a top example though, as cheap wines can be disappointing. Malbec is worth a fling for anyone serious about Merlot. Although this grape is from France, it has taken off spectacularly well in Argentina, making smooth reds, with plum and black-cherry and hints of chocolate.

Delight in the pleasures of fine Pinot Noir, with its silky smoothness and sensuous, perfumed strawberry fruit. But these are light on tannin. Then there's Sangiovese – the Tuscan grape behind Chianti. The rich, but slightly tart, red-berry character of Chianti Classico must surely appeal to all who love good Merlot. Indeed, it's interesting to note that if there is one type of wine that the Americans respect even more than Merlot, it's good classic Italian red. Both Chianti and Merlot are fruity and rounded, and both are consummately food-friendly.

Judging when to serve fine Merlot is tricky. Some of us prefer our top reds when they are relatively young, purple and sprightly, perhaps with some chewy tannins. Careful – you could be killing your wine off well before it has reached its peak. Others want to wait for their wines to mellow out, grow more brick-coloured, softer, more rounded. But again, watch out, as fruit flavours can fade.

when to serve

This is irrelevant in the case of all cheap, basic, and/or light Merlot, which is meant to be consumed almost as soon as possible. Medium-bodied Merlot will be ready to drink on purchase, but will keep perfectly well for a year or two, or in the cases of rather more full-bodied wines, three or four. Store in a cool, dark place, and rest the bottle on its side if keeping for long. So the dilemma of when to open Merlot only crops up with serious stuff – the top releases from the New World with plenty of structure and oak, top-quality Bordeaux, and robust premium Bordeaux-style blends from around the world. These benefit from ageing and may improve for twenty years or so after release. I would aim to open a top New World Merlot at five to seven years, and a good Bordeaux at nearer ten to fifteen. The best solution is to buy a case and try one bottle a year.

In almost all cases, Merlot should be served at room temperature. This doesn't mean placing it by the fireside for half an hour to "warm up" – this isn't room temperature at all and can bring out unappealing jamminess in the wine. Make sure your wine is no hotter than the room you are in. It's better to serve it slightly cold than slightly hot.

how to serve

In the case of the lightest, tangiest Merlot – one from Northern Italy, for example – a slight chill might actually benefit the wine, especially if you prefer to drink light reds, such as Beaujolais, served on the cooler side. Thirty minutes in the fridge will bring out the fresh, cherry-berry character of the wine. This won't be to everyone's taste, but it is well worth considering on a hot day when you want to enjoy a glass of mouthwatering Merlot.

Most Merlots and Merlot blends can be opened directly before serving. But the richest, most tannic types might need decanting before serving, either to aerate and mellow out the wine (simply removing the cork an hour before dining isn't adequate), or to remove a sediment that has collected at the bottom of the bottle. Pour the wine carefully and slowly into a glass decanter, and stop when the sediment appears. Use wide-bowled, plain glasses and only half-fill them to savour the aromatic liquid.

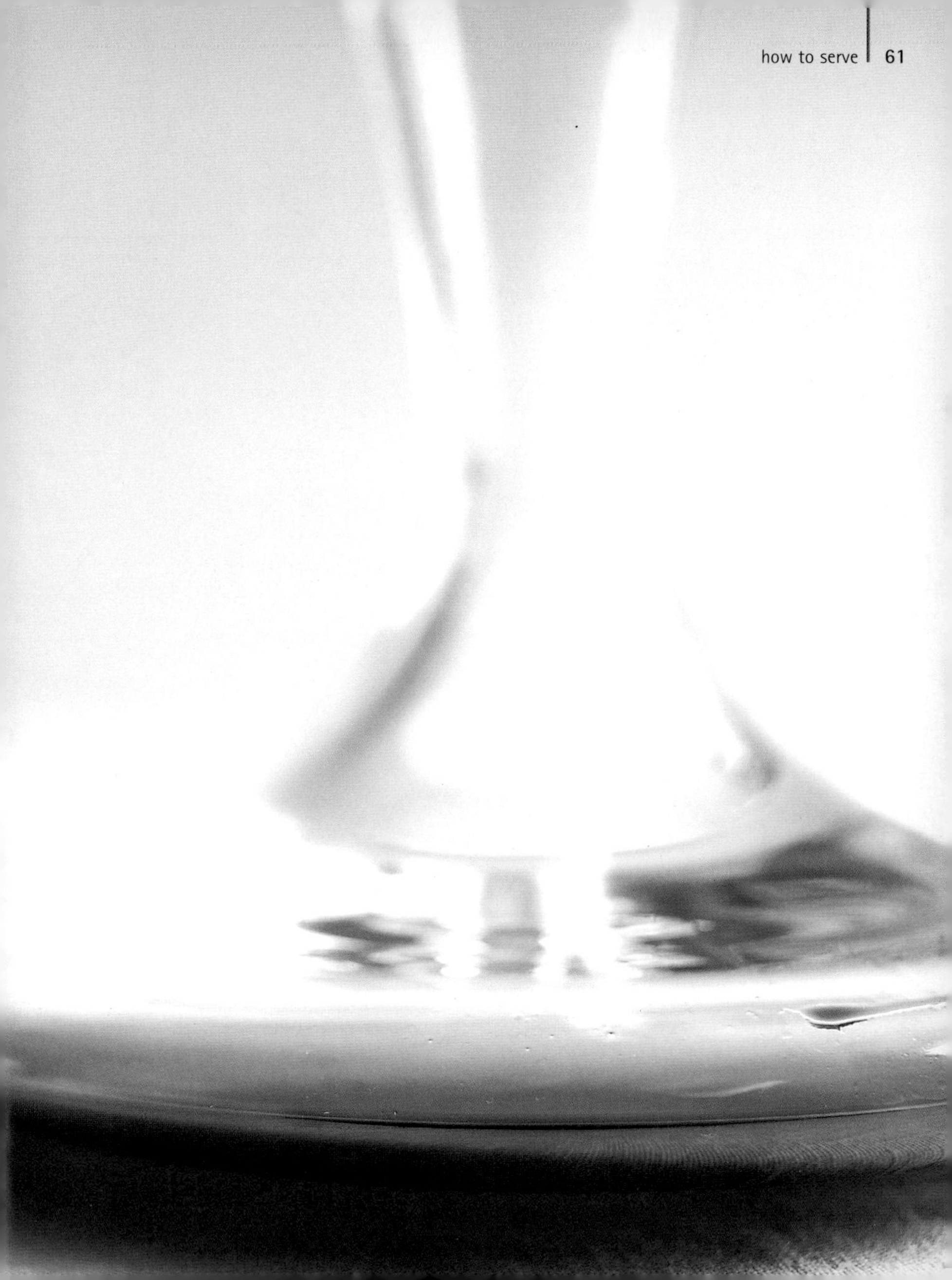

Wines made from the Merlot grape, or a blend of Merlot and Cabernet Sauvignon, for example, are among the most food-friendly reds you can buy. Try them with a wide range of dishes and see.

what to serve with

This grape tends to create well-balanced, medium-bodied wines and it has no "difficult" characteristics (such as loads of tannin or particularly high acidity, for example), that might clash with many recipes. So Merlot is a good choice if you are dining in a group and choosing several different items from a menu.

As a rule of thumb, pure Merlots and Merlot-based wines are best matched with roast poultry, steak, or game birds – particularly pheasant. They are also good with slightly sweet meats such as duck and ham, and with a wide range of medium cheeses (avoid the very mild, creamy or blue types of cheese). But a magical match depends on the style of your Merlot. So here are some more specific ideas:

Fruity, young, uncomplicated Merlot makes a great party wine, fine on its own, and for merrily washing down snacks like ham, sausage rolls, and pizzas. It goes well with supper dishes that include light tomato pasta sauces, too. Riper, juicier, somewhat fuller New World Merlots, perhaps with a hint of oak, are up to roast chicken or turkey, meats with a note of sweetness or a fruity sauce, like duck, pork, and ham dishes. They even go with medium-spicy curries (chicken, meat, vegetarian), and chilli con carne, too.

Bring out Merlot-rich clarets (red Bordeaux, see page 22) with game birds (either casseroled or roasted), venison, steak (again), and your best beef casseroles/stews/daubes. And with mature cheddar cheese or the best pâtés and charcuterie. They are not ideal with lamb, however, as it's the Cabernet component of claret that chimes in better here, so go for a Cabernet-heavy blend with dishes that use this particular meat.

index